Redeemed
Guide to Self-Love

By
Kristi Davis

©Redeemed Coaching 2021

Terms and Conditions
LEGAL NOTICE

© Copyright 2021 **Kristi Davis**

All rights reserved. The content contained within this book may not be reproduced, duplicated, or transmitted without direct written permission from the author or the publisher. Email requests to kevin@babystepspublishing.com

Under no circumstances will any blame or legal responsibility be held against the publisher, or author, for any damages, reparation, or monetary loss due to the information contained within this book, either directly or indirectly.

Legal Notice:

This book is copyright protected. It is only for personal use. You cannot amend, distribute, sell, use, quote, or paraphrase any part, or the content within this book, without the consent of the author or publisher.

Disclaimer Notice:

Please note the information contained within this document is for educational and entertainment purposes only. All effort has been executed to present accurate, up-to-date, reliable, complete information. No warranties of any kind are declared or implied. Readers acknowledge the author is not engaging in the rendering of legal, financial, medical, or professional advice. The content within this book has been derived from various sources. Please consult a licensed professional before attempting any techniques outlined in this book.

By reading this document, the reader agrees under no circumstances is the author responsible for any losses, direct or indirect, that are incurred as a result of the use of the information contained within this document, including, but not limited to, errors, omissions, or inaccuracies.

Published by Babysteps Publishing Limited All enquires to kevin@babystepspublishing.com

ISBN-13 9798459501841

Table of Contents

Why I Wrote This Book?

Looking back there were so many times I felt less worthy, unworthy, belittled, or depressed comparing myself to everyone around me. When you stop and think about what others, society, and marketing can do to a person, it is just so sad. Thinking we are not good enough; always wanting a differently shaped body, bigger and better this or that, the newest product or even social status. Thinking without it we are inferior. For so long I came across as happy but my smile masked the pain and I was never content. I knew that I was destined for something better, but I was not sure how to find it or how to get there. I reached a pivotal moment in my life when I realized happiness is not something that is external, it comes from within which is fed by the power-up above. It is not something money can buy or even words can fully explain.

I have been on this journey for almost 40 years. To some that is young and to some that is old, but I like to call it the sweet spot! The sweet spot is not an age, it's a point in life where you find this authentic peace that you have been yearning for. I love, however, that it is just that, a journey. With self-love and true happiness, there is no destination. Like a fine wine, it only gets better with time!

Over the years I have been blessed with being surrounded by some strong influential people. Some people helped lift me, others tore me down, but everyone had a purpose. I learned so many things; for one, EVERYONE is broken in this world. Everyone has insecurities or struggles with something. Knowing and acknowledging this has helped give them grace, not to jump to judgment, and strive to see something better within them. Growing up in the restaurant industry I became quite good at reading people and one of my favorite past-times is people watching. Trying to understand people and their stories.

I have been led down a career path I never thought I would be on but thank God every morning for. I spend my days connecting with some of the most amazing souls from all over the world and helping them on their journey of creating the best version of themselves that they can be. I am so honored that you are taking the time to read this book. Within these pages I share with you my journey, parts of my story, and some wisdom; in hopes that you can walk away feeling more grateful and enjoy that sweet spot in life too!

Why Should You Read This Book?

Whether you are turning on the TV or going on social media it seems the world is full of negativity, hate, gluttony, and corruption. However, there is so much more love happening than you may know. They say changing the world can be a ripple effect. The action that we can take for one person can change their world and they can create a ripple and change a life for others. Society and so many people I know were hit hard by the isolation and the hatred seeming to hit its peak in 2020. Depression, anxiety, abuse, and suicide are at an all-time high. More seem to be living a life of fear than leading a life of faith. I want to help breathe life and love into others. We need to stop looking to outside sources for our happiness and realize we have the power of choice, and it is a light that we can unlock within ourselves to shine for others to see.

There are several different avenues of what can create true happiness. Within these pages, I lay out the different areas in life that have found to be the most beneficial when you consciously focus your energy and time on them. Then you too will see some amazing positive changes occur.

Chapter 1.

Through him all things are possible

I understand everyone has their own beliefs and different levels of connection to a higher power. Based on cultures, religions, and backgrounds it is called different names including God, Spirit, Universe among many others. Whatever you resonate with, own it and let it grow within you to find your peace, love others and allow yourself to become the best version of yourself! Some of my best friends are Buddist, pray to Mother Earth, and manifest to the Universe. I respect and honor them. I personally love the Lord our father Jesus Christ and am also spiritual, believing we can not understand the magnitude of God with our human minds. If the concept of a higher power is new to you, I recommend that you reach out to people, research, and start to explore what is in your heart.

I grew up Christian, in the Catholic religion. My family did not attend church often, typically on Christmas, Easter and the few times a year our mom would force us all to go to church. For the most part, I was always a believer in God and Jesus Christ but anytime I would ask questions to leaders of the church in order to understand more, I would get shot down and told to "just believe." Throughout my teenage and young adult years, I strayed away from the church even more. I yearned for a connection but with every church, I would try to attend I felt like I didn't belong to the country club environment. I developed a bitter taste towards religion and felt some were very hypocritical. I believed in God and strived just to be a good person in life. I knew God was great but had learned churches can actually hurt people.

2016 was the turning point in my faith. We moved to a small town in northern Wisconsin and were struggling as parents to our amazing but very strong-willed son. We knew that something had to change for our family. I heard about this small non-denominational Christian church and talked my husband into attending. From the moment we walked through the door we knew it was different, it felt so warm and welcoming. We started to attend services every week and felt this incredible light growing within us. I started to understand there is a difference between believing in God and having a relationship with him. Looking around I started to realize everything in my world was an amazing blessing from the Lord that I did not give him enough credit for.

There was a certain message one Sunday morning about releasing your troubles to God. Now mind you, I have always had control issues; this formed what felt like a weight on my back of stress I carried around. Feeling like I had the power to get things done or everything would fall apart. I still vividly remember closing my eyes that day and picturing taking off this heavy backpack that I had been carrying around for so long and releasing it to God. The intense peace that moment brought was one of the best days of my life. It was the day Christians would say I was born again. I realized religion and faith did not have to be this hard confusing thing, it could be fun and freeing as I would walk in the grace of God.

Life was different from that day on. When I started to feel stressed or overwhelmed, I gave it to God. I no longer ever felt alone or hopeless. As my relationship with the Lord strengthened I started to see more of my life in so many ways shine. My relationship with my family improved my appreciation for my life, where I lived, and even the pride I had for myself. I was not as quick to jump to judgment or anger either. I was finding peace, peace I had always been yearning for. It has been a wonderful gradual journey that continues to get stronger over time. I am far from where I want to be but I know it will only continue to become more solid as I practice focusing on what I really have power on and truly what God has power over.

Once I started living a life of faith over fear I understood what it was like to actually live and not just be alive in a world of stress. I now try to make a conscious effort not to use words like fear or anxious when talking about my life or my situations. The words that we use can have a profound impact on us and how we look at situations. If I am feeling fearful or anxious, I acknowledge it but then remind myself if I am using those emotions then I am not trusting in the Lord as he already has a plan for us. It will work out the way that it is intended to work out. I must not fear or be nervous but instead lean into him, pray and have trust. When I do that, I find peace. I now like to say if I am feeling fear regarding something I am being called to do, such as writing this book, I make a conscious effort to switch to a sense of trust. Trust that God will breathe the right word to me, and place this book into the right hands that need to hear this message. When looking at our lives with a calming sense of trust it is hard for the negative emotions to penetrate us.

Do things always work out the way that we hope and pray for? Heck no, and looking back to some of the boys I dated and prayed I'd marry, I thank God that he had other plans for me! As humans, we have the power of choice but only if it was destined for us, it will happen. I like to say what if all prayers were answered on the other side of closed doors, but it is up to us to take the actions to open the doors in order to receive them. If we take action and it doesn't work out the way we wanted we almost always learn a lesson. Then we can proceed to open another door that was meant to work out. Learning to be still and hear what God is putting on our hearts to follow is important, feel what actions are needed and what is destined for us. Some may call that intuition, our conscience, or gut instincts.

There was a day I remember driving down the road and being in awe of one of the most beautiful sunsets I had ever seen. It was so phenomenal I actually had to pull the car over to take a picture of it. As I sat mesmerized by the beauty of the vibrant orange bursting from the earth's shining district rays of light for miles through the electrifying pink and purple sky, I got this amazing epiphany. We never look at a sunset and criticize it. We don't pick it apart and think well if there was pinker there or a longer ray of light on the other side then it would be much better. No, we take it in and fall in love with it for the beautiful work of art that God made it to be. So why don't we look at ourselves the same way? God created us with the same beauty as that sunset. There are no two identical. How wonderful is that? This hit me so hard, why would I waste my time wanting to be like anyone else? God made me to be me!

I was always what some would call a go-getter but after having this huge realization my world opened! I don't have to live in the box that society or others have told me I needed to be in. It was now my time to step it up and truly live the amazing life I had been given and treasure the body that I was blessed with. Once my trust was in the Lord I started to push myself outside my comfort zone. Realizing the only limits in life are what we put on ourselves. If God put something on my heart it is because he created me with the talents to do it and he will provide. I believe our talents are gifts from God but what we do with them are our gifts back to God. I hope as

12

God looks down at my life he smiles. He knows I am not perfect but strives to do all things with a good heart and when the day comes I meet him in heaven I hope he says well done my child.

At night, when driving down a dark road, you can only see your headlights shining 200 feet ahead of you. Yet you trust that the road continues beyond that. You trust that the road will lead to your destination and you will get there if you just continue to follow the beams on your car as they light the way. So why is it so hard for us to trust that God is lighting our path in life for us? We worry about what's going to happen weeks, months, and years down the road. What if we just focused on today, what decisions we can make to help improve our current situation, what prayers are being answered, and what tasks can be completed to put us in a better place for tomorrow. Take action and trust that God will continue to light the way and provide the path so we can reach our goals and accomplish what we are being called to do.

Chapter 2.

More than THANK YOU

Every November in America we celebrate the holiday Thanksgiving. We gather with our family and prepare a huge traditional meal. While sitting around the table, we take turns having each person explain what they are thankful for, it is always so touching to hear what everyone says. It has become a running joke in my family that I would always go last since I would take so long. But, I have so much to be thankful for! It would feel like the Oscar winners who won't get off the stage despite the exit music playing. I would talk about my wonderful, supporting, smart and talented husband, Jason. My amazing, funny, creative son, Apollo. My best friend and sister Tina, my great parents, extended family, friends, home, job, and so on. I would get choked up by all that I have to be thankful for. However, for years after the meal, the warm feeling would then take a back seat and reality returned to the hustle of life. Some may only take one day a year to stop and give thanks for all that is in their lives, some have rarely or never done this. I want people in my life to know how important they are to me every day and how much I love them. I made it a point to start telling people more often what they meant to me and that I appreciated them.

Showing appreciation seems so simple and yet often goes unsaid or unnoticed. Along my journey, I saw the negative effects when there was a lack of appreciation. Think about it, when you are not feeling appreciated at work, you start not to care. I had been on both ends of this over the years when it came to falling out of friendships, intimate relationships, and professional working relationships. There were times I was selfish and only thought about my needs; others when I felt like I gave and did so much without any sort of acknowledgment. I would shut down and things would start to fall apart. After the divorce from my first husband (I like to call it my practice marriage) I learned what I truly wanted and needed in a spouse. When I was blessed to meet the man I now get to call my husband, I did not take the great things he does for granted. I make

15

it a point daily to tell him how much I love and appreciate all he does for our family. In turn, he genuinely expresses the same back to me. Appreciation gives us both a sense of teamwork and acknowledgment for all the big and little things we do to create our life together. Especially those responsibilities that sometimes make us feel overwhelmed. I believe appreciation is a huge action we can do to show someone how we love them. Too often we feel taken advantage of by kids, partners, family, friends, and employers. Wouldn't it be a breath of fresh air to be shown more appreciation? If yes, do you think others around you feel the same?

Please understand that appreciation goes beyond "thank you." If you truly appreciate something and someone, take a moment to look them in the eye and say "I really appreciate...XYZ" The endorphins that will be released within the person you are talking to will be powerful and they will feel this as genuine.

A word and action that so many successful and happy people reflect regularly is GRATITUDE. The more we focus on something the more we see it. Let's take a moment and do an exercise… look around the room you are in right now. How many items in the room are green? Now come back to this page and say the number of purple items. Wait, you have no idea because you were not focusing on purple, right?!? Our brains create energy where we focus. So if we spend the day looking for good things in life that is what we will see. Where we can give gratitude, what is the positive in what is happening? The more things to be grateful for you will start seeing and before you know it, a lot more amazing things will be happening for you and around you. By taking time in expressing gratitude, you will instantly feel more fulfilled, satisfied and happier.

I once heard the saying, "what if we only had today what we thanked God for yesterday?" In turn, what if we only had tomorrow, what we thank God for right now….
I urge you to take a moment and reflect on that. What are you thankful for? People in your life, home, car, pets, job… What about the gift of life and the air that is filling your lungs? I now make it a daily practice every morning when I wake up, I place my hand on my

heart and thank God I woke up, since he woke me up, I have a purpose to live out. I reach over and thank God for my husband waking up, my son, my family/friends that come to mind, our dogs, my home, nice warm bed, the safety of where we live, so on and so forth, whatever comes to mind. I even have thanked God down to the socks that keep my feet warm. This starts my day with such a sense of love, and contentment in my heart that I then can't help but smile.

I one time had a client do this exercise to help her start focusing on gratitude. She had become such a negative being that it was hard for her to think of anything to be grateful for. So I mentioned her car, she started complaining about how it was a piece of junk and wanted to get a better one. However, when I began to ask questions about what her world would look like without a car, it switched her mindset. How would she get to work? How she would transport her daughter, changed her energy and she started to see that her car was a blessing and so were so many other things in her life that she had taken for granted. Showing us where we place our focus becomes where our energy goes either good or bad. We can complain that there is a sink of dirty dishes or we can be thankful that we had food to eat.

It is even in the words that we use. "**I have to** go to work" sounds like a punishment and weight on our day but if you "**get to** go to work" how exciting. You have the opportunity to make money so you can pay your bills and continue to live where you live, support your family, pay for your car and eat nice meals. That sounds like something you want to do. People don't say "I have to go to my favorite sporting event." They want to, they choose to because it makes life better. Everything is a choice in life. Very few things you "have to do" Try to be aware of this the next time you make a "have to" comment. Does it bring you to a state of dread or a state of gratitude?

Chapter 3

You are who you hang with

Please know that there is a difference between the people that we spend our time with and happiness. Happiness comes from within you, you create it. Then the people you choose to be around either add to it or start to suck it out of you!

Let's take a moment, think of and write down the top 4 people you spend the most of your time with; co-workers, your partner, friends, family, kids, etc. Now think of 3 words that honestly describe each of those people good or bad. Whichever top 3 words first come to mind.

1. _____; _____,_____,_____
2. _____; _____,_____,_____
3. _____; _____,_____,_____
4. _____; _____,_____,_____

Looking at these twelve words, could someone use them to describe you? If your best friend that you spend hours with on the phone is full of drama, then does your life have some drama in it? If you have a co-worker that is always complaining about work, do you have a lot of negative feelings about your job as well? If you are around anger and fighting, do you also find yourself yelling? You are so greatly influenced by who you surround yourself with.

Here is the list that I completed for myself:
Jason/husband- hardworking, supportive, creative
Apollo/son- strong-willed, silly, sensitive
Tina/sister- considerate, compassionate, loving
Lisa/friend- inspiring, motivating, strong

Looking over this list, yes I would think these words also describe me. These people in my circle do bring out the best in me.

This was not always the case. There were plenty of seasons in my life where I was around untrustworthy, negative, and very unmotivated people which led me to be the same. They were going in a different direction than where I wanted to be. I learned in my journey of self-love that if you are not around genuine, kind, inspiring people then you aren't striving to live your best life. Currently in my circle of friends and influence are wonderful people. We go to church with them, professionals, leaders, and volunteers in our community. They have all gone through some hard times in one way or another but have found a way to rise and live their best lives as well. That is what makes being around them so uplifting. We talk about ideas and encourage each other. There is no tearing down, ridiculing, or comparison. We cheer for each other and others with no jealousy.

If you are finding yourself in a season with people in your circle that don't inspire you, ask yourself why and take time to reflect on how you got here. Knowing that everything and everyone our time is spent with is a choice. I understand creating distance can be very hard especially if that person that brings some toxins into your life is a family member but then try and spend time finding people that do inspire and lift you up. Do you know any inspiring positive people? Start talking more to them. Create a new friend, reach out and start creating positive contacts on uplifting Facebook groups, join a personal development class, hire a life coach. Whatever you can do to start creating those influences in your life it just may help raise your positivity in life.

"You can't change people around you but you can change the people around you" -Anonymous

There was a point during the transition of leaving my corporate position and moving into my full-time personal development coaching business that I wanted to feel more encouraged and fired up. I created a goal to meet 30 inspiring people in 30 days. I knew in order to keep my energy high I needed to surround myself with some of the highest motivating people I could meet. I put out invitations on uplifting Facebook groups and hit my goal! I met people from all over the world thanks to the advancement in technology. They were from all different backgrounds and professions. I only counted the people that truly inspired me after hearing their story and what they had overcome while seeing their drive to achieve it. It encouraged me even more than I could have imagined. That was such a fun goal I set for myself and still keep in touch with so many of them today.

The circle of people we surround ourselves with can either help us rise like a hot air balloon or drag us down like an anchor. The choice is all ours. Are you setting standards for the type of people you choose to influence you? More than just the people we interact with influence us. You may not realize it but you are influenced by so much every time we go on social media, watch or read the news, the music we listen to, shows and movies we watch and books we read. I made it a point years ago to stop watching and reading things that didn't make me feel good. I called it my happy little bubble but now I like to say the greenhouse I live in since there is so much growth happening within me. Some may say I'm naive but I don't care. Was I informed as to what was happening in the world, yes but there was no need to sit and watch the 24-hour news stations. I stopped watching scary movies and cut out drama or negative people I had on social media. I even started to become more aware of the feeling I got when listening to different types of music. I now like to listen to worship music (never in a million years did I think that this would have become my preference) but whenever I listen to it, I feel lifted up, positive, peaceful, and encouraged. I enjoy my happy little greenhouse and have gotten to a point with lots of self-reflection to not care if people have a different opinion of me.

This was not always the case. I used to care what people thought of me, like really care. Being the heavy girl back in school I would constantly compare myself to others. I would think only if I was thin, better in sports, or had nicer clothes then I would be popular. I would always be so self-conscious in a group of people. Others wouldn't have known this since I was considered the class clown but I felt I would rather have people laughing with me than at me. This became my defense mechanism. Deep down I always felt like I was being judged for my appearance and I had to conform to

21

be accepted. Looking back, I wasted so much time caring instead of just living! I often say that we spend our entire 20's undoing what high school did to us. The day we stop giving a shit what people think of us is so freeing. Then you get to the point where you realize no one was thinking about you anyways since we are all just living in this self-conscious world and only thinking about what others think of us! Ugh, what a waste of time!

In life, you will always be "too much" for some people. Too loud, too soft, too this, or too that, but know when you stop trying to please and just surround yourself with the right people. They too will love you for who you are. Now when I walk into a room I don't worry about what people might think of me, I strive to create the energy in the room to help others feel comfortable and welcomed. I always say I may not be everyone's cup of tea but I am somebody's double shot of whiskey!

We really do have the ability to create the energy in the room and often underestimate the power of a genuine smile. Smiling at someone helps them feel more at ease and welcomed. You then appear more approachable and the energy in the room becomes lighter. If you are wanting to help create a shift of energy in the room you can, put your ego on the shelf for a moment. Go up to a person, start asking about them. People love talking about themselves so you showing interest in what they have to say will create a friendlier environment. We create change by shining like a lighthouse. People will be drawn to you and it will not only improve your day but theirs as well.

Part of the key to happiness is to understand the glass is not only half full but refillable and if needed you can even upgrade to a larger glass!

Everyone has a bad day but when you work in the service industry it is an unspoken rule that you are not allowed to ever be in a bad mood. Especially when I worked for tips as a waitress being in a bad mood affected by pay! So, I would use the saying "fake it until you make it." I would walk into work sometimes wiping tears from my eyes and throw on that fake smile. People that were close to me said they could even tell when something was wrong as the tone of my voice was even an octave higher. I put all of my energy into trying to act happy. However, without a doubt every time I had to do this by the end of my shift I was honestly in a better mood. The smile that I forced became genuine since I was telling myself I was in a good mood and it became more of my reality.

*This is just a tip to turn your day around but it is important to use your voice and distance yourself in a situation that is not healthy or continues to cause you distress.

Chapter 4.

YOU TIME- is not selfish it's love

As kids, we are taught never to be selfish, always give, share and think of others. This is true to a point, but we do need to think about ourselves too! The person we talk to most and will be with the longest is ourselves! I have always been a giver, one of my core values is still to serve others but I have learned we need to make ourselves a priority to be able to serve and help others. I like to picture we are all leaky buckets, like I said before, we are all broken in some way. As we leak and pour out for others, if we do not have a supply pouring back into us we will run out and burn out. For so many years I was trying to pour out of an empty bucket. Giving and giving so I would not come across as selfish trying so hard to people-please and have everyone like me.

On my quest to find activities to take care of myself and fill my bucket I looked around to see what others were doing. A lot of my friends would go to the gym or go for a run, they said it made them feel great and they were almost addicted to it. Well let me tell you, that is an addiction that never got a hold of me. I would go to the gym and work out watching the clock until it was time to leave. I did not want to be there. I would find myself walking on the treadmill watching the food channel, seems a little counteractive now looking back. I wanted to find the love of running that others were talking about. But being 250+ pounds and 5'5" it wasn't easy. I would joke when running next to my friends with their long lean legs that would glide gracefully compared to my short Oompa Loompa legs trying so hard to keep up. For over a year I would get up at 4:00 am and run 4 miles. I did 5k and 10k runs for that damn metal and banana at the end but never did I find the love in it as others talked about.

I yearned for that love for something that was so good for the body. I got into martial arts. Again I felt I didn't belong, I was too big and my body just didn't have the coordination, power, and flexibility needed. So, a yellow belt was my departing gift. I tried cross fit, thinking that would be my answer since I was always strong. But, after months of feeling like I was paying to get beat up and then not being able to walk or climb stairs for several days after class, it was not my thing either. I am not knocking ANY of these activities. My point is they just weren't right for me. I didn't want to give up. I wanted to find that activity that I could do for myself, to keep my body mobile as I age and help me lose weight.

I remember thinking "what is something that is good for my body that is also good for my soul?" I thought of yoga. This was something so new and foreign to me. In our small northern town, we did not have a yoga studio. I had never taken a yoga class and only seen peaceful pictures of people in different poses to have an idea of what it was. I have always been somewhat flexible, I thought maybe that would be something to try. I pulled it up on YouTube and did a session. MAN, IT BLEW my mind! I loved it! I found myself looking forward to doing it daily, an activity that I genuinely enjoyed, not one ounce of dread when thinking about doing it. The best part about yoga is anyone can do it at any fitness level. There is no comparison or competition with others but you can see the changes and advancements within yourself as you continue to do it.

I have now been doing yoga for almost two years. I have grown to love it so much that I became a certified instructor. I wanted to help others on their journey to find and fall in love with all the benefits of it. The best analogy of yoga I have ever heard is yoga is not to tighten your butt, it is to get your head out of it. Along with yoga comes meditation. Again in the fast-paced world, I was used to, I had no idea how to meditate. But once I started it became such an important practice to continue. It is an exercise for the mind. Training ourselves to be still and present in the moment.

At first, I felt guilty taking time away from family or things that I felt were more productive. But, once I found something I could do to help refill my bucket I knew I had to continue to do it for my sake and everyone around me. Self-care and maintenance are productive! You know the benefits of changing the oil in your car so why are we thinking that we don't have to take care of our bodies and minds? Taking the time to recharge is not selfish, it is necessary.

I encourage you to find something every day that is good for your soul and do it. I encourage you to ask yourself the question "what would be good for my soul" and then do it. Some days it can even be more mental and emotional than physical. Pick up a paint brush, write in a journal, play an instrument, or read a book that has been collecting dust on the shelf you have been yearning to read (thank you that it is not this one!!).

I have found the best and fastest way that I have been able to become more grounded in life, is to go out in nature. The amazing power of mother earth. Just tilt your head back, close your eyes, open your arms and take in a few deep breaths. The amazing feeling of the fresh air filling your lungs, so calming, so glorifying. Take off your shoes and walk in the grass. Listen to the birds. There really is something amazing and spiritual that happens when we connect with nature. To deepen this experience and bring yourself to the present moment I encourage you to take a few minutes and check in with your senses. Listen and see if you can hear five things, then look around and see five unique things, take some breaths in through your nose, what does it smell like, and last feel the grass and other items taking the time to feel it. Doing this practice regularly will allow you to slow your mind and truly live in the moment. Whatever activity it is that you choose, be sure the answer is yes when you ask "is it good for my soul."

Please don't make the excuse that you don't have time to do a soul-filling activity. There is more time in your day and week than you think. What are your time wasters? Let's see…social media scrolling or what about binge-watching TV? If you still feel like every moment of your life is scheduled and there is no time for any activity that is good for the soul I would say 2 things; is there something that you could cut out of your day that is not serving your soul or suggests you wake up earlier in the morning. That's right, set your alarm! Even 30 minutes earlier will make a big difference. There are so many studies that show if you have a healthy morning routine that includes reflection, meditation, and body movements it has a huge impact on your day. So when the alarm goes off, you can either stay in bed and dream or get up and live the dream life you create. The choice is yours.

My husband and I have created a great morning routine that we both cherish. The resort wakes up and things start moving at 8:00 am; so we wake up at 6:00 am to start our day. We spend two hours together, talking over our morning coffee. No electronics, just us. We talk and truly connect, update each other on what has been happening and often discuss our goals. Sometimes we go for a walk but it is a priority for us to stay connected and I feel this time together is a huge contributor to our strong and happy marriage. Our schedules are very busy so there are not a lot of date nights but we have date mornings every day and it is so good for the soul. We then go on with our tasks needed for the day but having started the day this way we feel grounded, connected, and stronger mentally.

Chapter 5.

Find your purpose

While in high school, I got decent grades but I never wanted to go onto a traditional college. Again high school was not my happiest years and I did not want that social environment to continue. I couldn't afford it and didn't know what I wanted to do in life anyway; so I entered the workforce. I worked at a bank then worked briefly in direct sales. Nothing seemed to be a fit so I went back into waitressing since that is what I did throughout my high school years. I enjoyed it but had this crazy idea to have my own restaurant.

When I was twenty-two years old I decided it would be a great idea to build and operate a restaurant and that is exactly what happened! I called my sister and pitched her this crazy idea, she was all in! Back in 2004 when banks were lending money like water we got a loan and built a family-style restaurant in our small hometown. The stress level that we felt was through the roof. We felt we had to always keep a smile on our faces, had to keep everyone happy from the customers to employees and know all of the answers. The countless hours working and utter exhaustion lead to a lot of stress, so many tears, and alcohol. I would stay during the night after the restaurant closed to make wedding and unique birthday cakes. Anything we could do to keep the restaurant afloat. We became completely burnt out after seven years. There was not one drop left in mine nor my sister's bucket. We could not recover from the deviation from the 2009 economic crash and had to make the hard decision to say goodbye to the restaurant we had poured our love and lives into. After filing bankruptcy and ending with the same nothing we started with, it was hard but it was the right choice. Looking back now, I can't believe we did it. We were so young and had no idea what we were doing but we took a leap of faith and ran that restaurant with all of our heart and soul. We learned so much during that period of time. When we think back we laugh and shake our heads at what those years brought. We do not regret doing it one bit!

During the final years of the restaurant days, I met my current husband. He was so supportive and encouraging after we closed for me to "find myself." This was a task so much easier said than done. All I knew was work, my identity was the sister from the restaurant. But I started to take time to discover who I was and who I was created to be. This was a ten-year process and I still continue to find pieces I didn't know existed. I started volunteering at the humane society and meals on wheels with the elderly community. However, I quickly found myself volunteering over forty hours per week so I had to reevaluate and took a management position in retail. I then took an entry-level position in the claims department of worker' compensation insurance. This was not what I would define as my purpose but I learned a lot about myself, I was good at it and enjoyed the salary that came with it as I accepted promotions.

During this time I became a mom, what a beautiful and stressful journey that was! My husband and I can not have children due to medical reasons and we were fine with just dogs for several years. After the realization of how many children grow up in and age out of America's foster care system, we knew we had to do something and stepped up. We decided to adopt from the Wisconsin foster care system and in 2014 our spunky four-year-old son came into our life. Becoming a mom has brought out so much in me that I didn't think was possible. Our life was completely flipped upside down but the massive love that grew for our son formed a piece of my heart that I never knew was missing.

During a promotion process in my insurance career days, we moved our family to our small northern town in Wisconsin. My husband and I embarked on an amazing and some would say crazy journey. On a whim, we bought a run-down lake property that once was run as a resort. We took a leap of faith, rolled up our sleeves, and completely renovated and updated the four year-round cottages and a house; creating a thriving business we call Tomahawk Resort on Lake Alice www.tomahawkresortwi.com

We had to learn the hospitality industry quickly but knew if we treated people well and provided great accommodations it would make for a successful business. It has now been five years, several of our recurring guests have become like family to us. We love the life that we have created. Yes, it is a busy life and never a dull moment but we are so happy that we made this decision. The saying goes create the life you don't need a vacation from, and we really have.

The piece that was still not making me happy and sucking my soul was being in corporate America. I felt I was in jail, tied to my desk for forty-plus hours a week. Being drained with a job that was not my purpose. I kept at it for so many years for the pay but soon the thought of being fully fulfilled spending my days living out my purpose of serving people far outweighed the security I felt I had at a desk. I had to look deep within myself and discover who I was and what I was meant to do. I had been working on my own personal growth to find true happiness for many years. As God always does, he puts the right people in your life when they are meant to be there. I had made changes in my diet to work on my health. I started to be asked by friends and family what I was doing and to help them with their eating habits and issues with food dependencies.

Helping others in this way fed my soul. Seeing them succeed was so rewarding. I decided to obtain my certification as a vegan nutrition health coach. I started small with friends and family but wanted to grow a business. Subsequently, I was approached and started helping several friends and acquaintances through hard times they were having, being there to listen, moral support, and help give some advice.

I had become known as the positive person that helped others see things from a different perspective. One of my close friends planted the seed of me becoming a life coach. Honestly, I had no idea what that even was. After looking into it I knew that this was exactly what I was created to do! I found a wonderful coaching school and took the leap to invest in myself. I have since graduated from the Insight Coaching Community and am a certified life coach. This was one of the best decisions I have made and have found my purpose.

I now work with clients one on one and in group coaching settings. I worked hard to build this new business. I set out to find what I was made to do and be fulfilled in all aspects of my life. I did it, I have since left the corporate insurance world to pursue my passion and purpose of helping people with personal development and health coaching. I have brought so many of my passions to host personal retreats at the resort including custom yoga, nutritional cooking classes, and personal development courses.

When we think of what our purpose in life is it can become overwhelming. I always was afraid I'd get it wrong but when we are being called to do something by the Lord he also helps create a path to make that calling into a reality. Discover your purpose, pursue your purpose. For the years I have spent studying happiness the root comes back to having a purpose. Even big-name celebrities that *make it* on so many levels say they are still not happy. However, people that find their true purpose and continue to live it out, while evolving, report feeling genuinely happy.

Are you at a loss as to what your purpose is? Take some time and reflect. What have you experienced or done in life that you really enjoyed? Think about places you've gone, jobs you've held, or people you've helped. Has there been something put on your heart that you are being called to do? Even if it seems huge or crazy to pursue it, it very well may be part of your purpose. Is there a topic that lights you up and you could spend hours reading about it or talk about it to a complete stranger? When do you feel the most comfortable? You can live out the life you were destined for. Again we are not all the same so your path should look different than those around you. If you are not feeling supported by people in your circle as you discover what your purpose is, I encourage you to re-read chapter three!

If you're not living out your purpose, your desire to change must be greater than your desire to stay the same. Remember, there are people less qualified than you that are making it, the difference is they decided to believe in themselves and go for it! Be inspired and take action too.

Chapter 6.

Living a life of no regrets

As you understand and feed into your purpose now it is time to act on what you have been created to do. Are you spending your days feeling fulfilled with all that life has to offer or are you spending days counting down to the weekend or vacation time? Yes, we need to work to earn money but it's how we earn that money that is what is important. When working in a job that was not my purpose I would look forward to Friday at 5 o'clock. That was when I felt like I was free and the world was mine, Saturday would go by way too fast and by Sunday evening I had a pit in my stomach knowing Monday was fast approaching and dreaded what the week would bring. This went on for years.

When I started putting the time and effort into my personal development and growth to live an authentic life of happiness this dread and a black cloud were even more apparent because I was becoming more aware of what fed my soul and understanding the great feeling of peace and happiness. I had gotten to a point where I earned more money than I ever thought I could in the corporate world. If I just found another job it would mean taking a pay cut. I knew if I was going to create true fulfillment and happiness I had to think outside of the box. I had always had an entrepreneur soul so why not build on that? I put time and thought into what I would want to do all day long that would not feel like work but be a rewarding successful business and here we are.

I still remember when I was twenty-one, while married to my first husband I was so unhappy. I was diagnosed with depression, placed on medication, and started seeing a therapist. A friend of ours was diagnosed with cancer and told she had six months to live. That honestly was my wake-up call. I asked myself if I had only six months to live would I be happy with the way I spent my last six months? My answer was a loud NO! It snapped me out of a sense of feeling stuck and into a sense of urgency. If I was not happy, then why was I allowing myself and my situation to stay this way? I did not want to let the months turn into years and years turn into decades; only to become this miserable old married couple that fought constantly while being kept in a state of fear from the abuse.

Making that huge transition and change was scary but at the same time, it was the most freeing feeling I have ever had. I could breathe again. I felt happy for a change and it wasn't the medication. I was able to stop taking medication altogether and no longer needed the therapy. I started living a life that was for me. I am of course not a doctor or an expert on this matter, this is just my situation that led me to believe that sometimes in life when I am feeling constantly down, stuck or miserable it might not be a chemical imbalance but a circumstance. Meaning if I change how I'm living life then I will feel more fulfilled, happy, loved and that is what is needed for me versus a prescription.

This was not the way I wanted to live and I did not have to stay in this dark hole that I had convinced myself that I was trapped in. I understood if something was going to change I had to make the change and a big change I made. I left everything, the job that I was at, the house we bought, all of my possessions and I left my husband. I moved back home to my parents and came clean to my family about the toxic marriage that I was in and the mental state that I was working to get out of.

A lot of times we question ourselves or even others such as "why would they buy that or do that…" I like to respond with the phrase "why not." Why would they paint their house pink? Why not? Why would they spend their money on that? Why not? We live in a world of judgment on others and ourselves. Being taught from a young age to fit inside of this box society calls normal. But what really is normal and if everyone was the same how boring would that be? Living a life of our true authentic self is a must. A good friend of mine uses the word authentic regularly and I love that about her. It helps me stop and think about what makes me and my life authentic? We all strive to be genuine and unique, true to ourselves but are we living out our life that way or are we judging others and ourselves trying to fit into the box?

We can set goals and tell ourselves one day but know one day is not guaranteed. People that passed away today had plans for tomorrow. We save for retirement but then often use retirement as the destination to start living. Yet so many don't make it to retirement. When are we going to stop saying "one day" and start saying "today!" Have you been holding off on making a decision? Making a big change? A big move? Going on a dream vacation? How about you stop shoving it off until one day and start taking steps to create that dream into a reality? When there is a will there's a way and when it is your destiny God will open the doors.

Understanding every decision you make is part of your journey and your story. Everyone's story is different and has different chapters in them. Some sad, some happy but how about creating the exciting parts of your story and not just living in the safe spot. Looking back at your life, have you had opportunities you passed up that you regretted? Wouldn't it be wonderful to look back at your life and have a smile on your face while shaking your head thinking "man, I sure did live an amazing life?" So let's start now. If you woke up this morning and you are reading this, it is not too late! Every story has chapters and chapters come with change. What would you regret if you did not do it? Even if it is hard, embrace it. With every change, you learn more about yourself and grow into your authentic self. There is never the right time, only time.

So let me ask you… If you got the call that you only had six months to live, would you be happy with the way you spent your last six months? If not, why? What would you change? Who would be the person/people you would want to spend as much time with within these last six months? Are you making them a priority in your life now?

Take the time to live in the moment. Stop dwelling on the past, it is over. There is no need to worry about the future, for it is not here yet. Let's spend time living today! Show up with a full heart and true genuine intentions. The way we talk to others and who we spend time with is all a choice. It could be anyone's last day on earth. Take some time to reflect on the relationships in your life. If you never had a chance to speak to them again would you be at peace with how you spoke to them the last time you saw them? Tell people that you love them. Tell them how much they mean to you. Make sure there are no regrets about the way things might be left. Don't put yourself in a situation where you think you should have done something differently or only if you would have... make that action today. Mend a torn relationship if it has been weighing on you. Take the time to call your family and friends just to say hi and tell them how much you love them for it could be the last time you get to say it. Having this as a common practice, when we have to say goodbye to someone we can be at peace knowing they knew all that was on our heart or our mind.

Chapter 7.

RSVP no to the pity party

So often we hear people say life is hard, adulting is hard. Well, being overweight is hard but so is having a workout schedule and a healthy eating plan. Being married can be hard but so is being divorced. Being poor is hard but so is sticking to a budget. It is all about how we look at it. So stop throwing yourself a pity party! If you focus on the hard it will always be hard. When we focus on negative thoughts it actually changes our energy level and narrows our mind's ability to function and see all of the possibilities. Almost like looking through a pinhole. We throw ourselves into a state of mind where we don't see a way out of the dark hole we are putting ourselves into.

The words we use to speak to ourselves have so much impact on our mood. We talked before about using the words "have to" versus "get to" but there are so many other words and phrases we should be aware of when having self-talk. We talk to ourselves worse than we would talk to an enemy. The name-calling, the criticism, the self-doubt. Why don't we encourage ourselves the way we would encourage our children or best friends? We talk to ourselves more than we talk to anyone else so why not choose kind loving words?

NEW SELF-CARE:
TALK TO MYSELF
THE WAY I TALK
TO DOGS

"HI, SWEET GIRL."
"YOU'RE SO CHUBBY
AND CUTE."
"WANT A TREAT?"
"NEED A NAP?"

The next time you start judging and talking down to yourself I invite you to take a deep breath, and a moment to see what is really going on. Are you feeling overwhelmed? Is there a lesson to be learned? Is there a better way or healthier way to do something? Also, ask yourself the question, does it really matter? If you are getting upset about something that you won't even remember in a month from now then why are you letting it get you so worked up now? Are you doing a task that is not even needed and is not good for your soul?

Sometimes we get so wrapped up in the stories that we are telling ourselves and even blowing up in our minds for nothing. They are not even true! A great example is when someone you love is not answering their phone. You continue to try to call but time goes on and still no answer and no response. Our brain starts to spin and we start thinking of what could be going on. They fell, they were hurt, they were kidnapped, they are laying on the side of the road dead! We start to panic with all of the stories we are telling ourselves but in reality, they left their phone on silent and didn't hear it ringing while they were watching a movie. Our minds can go down destructive paths if we let the stories we tell ourselves lead the way.

How often do we overthink or replay possible situations over and over in our minds? So often going in a negative direction. To change this unhealthy cycle we need to stop and address the thoughts. Ask yourself, is this thought I am having a fact, or is it a story that I am telling myself. So often we are getting worked up over a story. If we let the story consume us it can be devastating, cause fights and even end relationships. No, your partner was not checking out that other person at the bar, they were looking at the clock to see what time it was and they are happy they get to go home with you. Or that lady that just looked at you up and down maybe she was admiring your outfit and your style. It is the negative thoughts we place on the situation that makes them feel like reality in our mind but not all of our thoughts are true! This has shown time and time again in my life as a hard lesson to learn.

The biggest example of this was a friendship that was torn apart based on a story that I had told myself. Just a few years ago my husband and I became really good friends with a new couple that had moved to our town. We had so much fun when we got together and grew close. We went to the same church and we're even planning to go on vacation together. But with a few events within our circle of friends, they left our church. I told myself that they thought they were better than us and felt used and betrayed. I had this bitterness that I was caring around for way too long. I hated this feeling and asked God for forgiveness and to grant me the grace to forgive them. I prayed they would find what they were looking for and receive what was needed to fulfill their lives. Of course, as God does he had a plan. Our paths cross again, the message in church that Sunday was to forgive and ask the person you have bitterness with for forgiveness.

We both heard that message and tears rolled down our faces. We started messaging each other and come to find out the same thing I was thinking is what my friend had been thinking! All this time we both were telling ourselves stories! So much time and energy wasted! We are now friends again and working to slowly build the type of friendship we had before. I love my friends so much and it hurts my heart to think that it was thrown away with just a story.

Start looking at the facts. You really are in charge of your own thoughts. Understanding and practicing this will help you refocus your mind and emotions, helping you get back on track with peaceful, healthy, and goal-orientated thoughts. A positive mind creates a positive life.

"Whether you believe you can or believe you can't you're right" -Henry Ford

Now that you realize you have control over your thoughts, understand that really your thoughts are your only limits. So often we want to do something, go somewhere or create something yet we are so quick to talk ourselves out of it and find the reasons it won't work. So what if we switch our thinking to we absolutely can do something and start thinking of the steps to make the desire a reality. A dream is merely a desire, something you can sit around all day

41

and fantasize about but you can make it into a goal by breaking it down and understanding the action steps needed to make it happen. So many people had a dream they turned into a goal and is now a reality. The difference is they controlled their thoughts in order to get it done. Therefore nothing will change until you choose to take steps to make your dreams your reality. You have so much more power than you give yourself credit for.

So when is a good time to start this new way of thinking and creating plans to turn your dreams into goals? NOW! Don't put it off until someday or tomorrow or even after you are done reading this book, Make it right now. Procrastination is the assassination of all of your goals. You don't need to know it all or even all of the steps. Just start where you are and grow from there. Remember God will light your path and put people and things in the near future to make your goals become reality but it is up to us to do the work!

Goals:_____

_____
_____
_____
_____
_____
_____
_____
_____
_____

Everyone's path is different. Often we waste time comparing ourselves to others. As we've discussed everyone is made to be different so let's be different! Your path and story shouldn't look like anyone else's. Finding happiness comes from within. Happiness is a choice and not a result. Nothing will make you happy until you choose to be happy. Your happiness will not come to you, it comes from you. No person will make you happy until you decide to be happy. You become what you focus on so start focusing on the possibilities and not the impossibilities.

This takes practice, like working a muscle at the gym. If you want to have ripped abs and only do a sit-up once in a while you'll never reach your goal. You have to be consistent. Make the time and the effort to do the work. Changing your mindset is very similar. Start by making yourself more aware of your thoughts, your negative self-talk, and your judgment either towards yourself or towards others. Once you heighten your awareness you can identify it and even stop it in the moment. Then redirect your thoughts to look at the facts. Take baby steps, but soon it will become easy and natural. Think of the positive and let it go.

Along with prayer, an influence in my journey and well known throughout the world is the term "Law of Attraction". When talking about our thoughts being our reality it is a must to introduce you to this concept. This first originated in the 1906 book when author William Walker Atkinson explained how our thought vibrations attract our reality. The popularity quickly grew in 2006 when Rhonda Bryne released the film "The Secret" interviewing several world philosophers and authors to explain the Law of Attraction and manifestation. Ultimately explaining whatever an individual's thoughts are, is what their reality creates. If you focus and your energy is on the negative then this will create more negative in your life. If you use positive uplifting words and thoughts this then becomes your reality. If you have not read this book or watched this film, I highly encourage you to do so.

Starting your day with affirmation or positive statements can be very helpful in setting the tone for the day. Even taking the time throughout your stressful day to reflect, read and resight your personal affirmation can reset your mind and turn around your mood. When creating your personalized affirmations be sure to use positive words and phrases such as "I am strong" not "I am not weak." Since you are still using the negative word it will still give it power and energy.

Here are some examples you may want to include in your daily affirmations:

I believe in myself and I am confident
I am successful with all challenges I face
I am authentic and will live out a happy life
I love and respect myself
I focus on the positive in situations

Redirecting your thoughts is not always an easy task. You may want to talk to the people in your circle and explain that you are starting to work on becoming more positive. Since there will be times you voice your negative thoughts or judgment they can help you recognize it.

With trying new things and working on staying more positive and grounded you may find you are getting some negative feedback from your friends and family. Remember misery loves company so if they are used to you gossiping or complaining about life with them and now you're practicing your new way of thinking they may not understand it. You may even feel you are being rejected by them. But if you feel rejected, know it is God redirecting either them to understand what you are trying to do or redirecting you to a new group of people that will understand you and love you for the clear-minded, calm, loving, happy person you are becoming.

Chapter 8.

Laugh, stop being so damn serious

Laughter is our birthright and a natural part of life. When we are infants we begin laughing within the first few months. When we are kids we laugh multiple times daily. Heck kids laugh at everything, they find joy in so much! Their laugh is genuine and contagious. But as we grow into the teenage years we start thinking we are too cool. That light and laughter start to fade. We are told to grow up and be serious. Life continues and laughter becomes rarer. I would like you to take a moment and think of the last time you had a good laugh, I mean a good, loud, make your belly hurt kind of a laugh. For some of us, we can not think of the last time. We can think of times that brought us joy but not busting a gut laughing.

There is a reason they say laughter is the best medicine. When we laugh it releases endorphins in the brain causing us to feel happier, puts us in a better mood, and can reduce stress hormone levels. It can even strengthen your immune system and diminish pain. Studies have shown nothing works faster to bring your body and mind back into balance than a good belly laugh. Laughing relaxes the whole body and calms the mind.

There are multiple social benefits to laughter as well. It attracts us to others when we see a group of people laughing. We want to be part of it and hear the joke as well. It can help defuse conflict. Sometimes in the heat of a conversation, someone can crack a joke and it reduces the tension that is being felt. It can definitely strengthen relationships, how often do you hear couples say they don't laugh anymore and their marriage is suffering? It almost seems like it goes hand and hand. The ability to include laughter also promotes teamwork. So why don't we make it an effort to laugh more often? Are you putting yourself in situations where you are around others and having a good laugh?

There is a difference between fun light-hearted comedy and laughing at someone. Please ensure that the laughter is not at someone else's distress. Everyone involved in the joke needs to find humor in it. If you find yourself feeling bad for the person at whom the laughter is directed at, it is not genuine joy that feeds the soul. Please either stick up for the person that it is focused on or turn it off and redirect your attention to something more kind and uplifting.

It is ok to laugh at ourselves too. I recall an evening when I was making dinner and the entire pot of spaghetti dropped and erupted, splattering all over the kitchen. My first instinct was to get mad and swear but I looked over and saw my son standing there with the biggest eyes in shock I have ever seen and his mouth hanging wide open by the mess that was just created. I couldn't help but burst out into laughter. At first, he was so confused but then he started to chuckle too. Soon we both had a good laugh and he then helped me clean up the kitchen. We have a choice of how to respond. I could have lost my cool, started yelling, and spent the next hour pissed off as I cleaned up the mess but I chose to make the best of it and laugh about it since there was nothing I could do about it anyhow.

Laughter is contagious. There's a reason why TV sitcoms use laugh tracks so we can join in. You are more likely to laugh with others. However, even if we are not surrounded by light-hearted, humorous people we can still find opportunities for laughter. We can watch a funny TV show, movie, or video on social media. Read the comics, a joke book, or visit the humor section at the library. You can play with a pet. If you don't have a pet, go volunteer at the humane society. Go to a comedy club or a hypnotist show. Some of the best belly laughs I have gotten were when seeing a good entertainer. Even the next day I was sore from laughing so hard! I always get a great belly laugh by watching my favorite actress, Melissa McCarthy's movies. This will always set me in a great mood. You can take an improv or comedy class. I was invited to take an improv class a few months ago by a coaching college of mine. Not knowing what to expect and thinking I would never see the people I was participating with again, I told myself not to hold back and enjoy it. I did, my face hurt so bad from laughing and smiling during that class. It brought such joy to my soul and I am looking forward to doing it again.

Really try to seek out and create a circle of friends that also like to laugh and engage with them by doing activities that will promote fun and laughter including hosting a game night. When we get together with our group of friends and play charades it takes everything in me not to pee my pants from laughing so hard! Make plans to do fun activities outside of the home too such as bowling, karaoke, and miniature golfing.

Sometimes reflecting on memories where we were living a life of no regrets brings the best form of laughter. It always seems when my husband gets together with the group of his high school friends they always have the best laughs talking about the good ol' days. You can not enjoy a laugh with people unless you are truly engaging with them. This means putting down your phone and interacting face to face. This is shown to be the highest form of laughter to rebalance the nervous system.

It's time to find and bring back your inner child. Stop taking your life and things so seriously. Pay attention to children, play, and enjoy interacting with them. Try and emulate them, their laughter and silliness will help bring out the joy and laughter in you. Who cares if you look silly. Maybe even if people are watching they may not be thinking negative thoughts, they could be envious of you, that you can let yourself be free and find joy in the little things.

Seize the moment, play make-believe, go swimming or even go dance in the rain with your children. Not only are you finding enjoyment in life but you are creating memories with your children. Let's teach our children that creativity and joy has no age limits.

47

Allowing yourself to be free is one of the most rewarding feelings. Our family would take a biannual trip to see my in-laws in North Carolina. Every time we went I would make it a point to go to the ocean to watch a sunrise. Something so magical happens when the light begins to glow over the water and hearing the sound of the waves crashing. I would walk on the beach and dip my toes in the water but I always just wanted to set myself free; do handstands and cartwheels. I would hold back thinking of how silly I would look and not know if my body could even do those movements without injuring myself!

My in-laws decided that they were moving back to Wisconsin to be closer to our family and we were going down to visit them one last time before the move. This was going to be the last time that I may see the ocean for the next several years. That's it, if I wanted to live out the joy that I felt in my heart I had to make it happen! So with only a few months before our vacation, I started to practice and work towards my goal of being able to set myself free at the beach! The time came, we made the trip and on the second day there, we traveled to the beach in the dark. It was a cold morning but I didn't care. My excitement rose with the sun. My husband knew my intentions and captured the moment. When my hand hit the sand and my legs came up I was so full of joy and laughter. I was living life full out. I kept going and going, not caring what any passerby was thinking. It was a wonderful day to remember and I will always cherish it.

Something I do regularly to keep my inner child free is to dance in the kitchen while cooking. I love to put on my favorite songs and bust a move! I get down and funky sometimes. Of course, this makes my now twelve-year-old son place his hand on his forehead and shake his head at me in embarrassment but it almost always leads to laughter. Dancing is so good for the soul and our bodies. As we age out of the nightclub life most people only dance at weddings and when they get to see a band play. But when was the last time you really gave it your all, popped all of those moves, and felt free dancing without any apologies? Just felt the music in your bones. If you can't think of a time I encourage you to let yourself be free and experience it! No one is watching!

Finding things that bring you joy and laughter are all around you; you just need to stop and live in the moment. Sing in the shower at the top of your lungs. Acts like you are trying out for American Idol. Most adults use shower time to think about all the tasks that need to be done for the day or replay situations in their minds. But why not take that time to create joy? Be silly, starting your day off with a smile. Switching your brain to be in a good mood really can set the tone for your entire day. So often we worry about what people will think or if they will judge us if we set ourselves free but the person putting the most judgment on you is you. Relax and find joy in the little things!

Chapter 9.

Saying "no" is a complete sentence

Looking back, I would say, I was always a people-pleaser. I would act a certain way to fit in. I would bite my lip as to what I wanted to say and just put a smile on my face to keep the peace.

It started as a young child. My parents were old school and we were raised that children are to be seen not heard. We were to do as we were told and we knew better than to back talk. When our parents or authority asked us to do something we didn't ask why, we just did it. This is how a lot of people I know were raised. Then in preadolescence, when we discover we have a voice and start to use it, we are told we are being disrespectful and to keep our mouth shut. So it's no shock that by the time we are an adult we are having such an internal battle when we need to stick up for ourselves or others!

Finding my voice was a big part of self-love and being happy. I can't count the number of times that I didn't speak up when I should have. Whether it was in a friendship, a working relationship, an intimate relationship, to my family, or even with complete strangers. I hate conflict. Just the thought of it made me tense up and want to retreat to avoid it. I didn't want to upset people, cause a fight or have people, not like me. How sad is that? Walking around on eggshells with a smile on my face while others walk all over me?

As the love for myself grew in turn, so did my confidence. I was not a doormat and did not deserve to be spoken down to by anyone. I don't talk down to myself so I sure was not going to let another human do it to me. As my strength grew and I came across situations I would normally retreat from I found myself facing it. The difference that I found though was I was not jumping to anger like I normally would feel and then suppress. Instead, I found myself so often feeling a sense of compassion or yearned for understanding what was making that person so upset. I would find myself making

51

eye contact and sometimes just be able to walk away but not from a place of fear but from a place of peace. It was just not worth my time or energy. When I use my words and voice I try to stay calm and explain my side of the situation. Then take time to listen to resolve. We may not always agree but sometimes we can agree to disagree. Several people in my life do not have the same beliefs as me. They hold different opinions on so many controversial topics. Society has become so divided because people get angry when others don't think the way they do. If we want people to respect us and our opinion we need to do the same for them even if we don't agree. Everyone has a reason they believe in what they believe even if you feel it is wrong. I urge you to take a moment and give them grace. If they are not hurting someone or inflicting pain then strive to understand and give them grace. Even if someone did hurt you, give them grace. Do not hold grudges.

Ultimately holding a grudge only continues to hurt you, not them! They have moved on with their life doing their thing and you continue to keep yourself in a place of pain holding onto that grudge. It's like hanging on to a hot piece of coal that someone had placed into your hands and then walked away. You can stand there and yell, cry and plead the pain but it is not until you let it go and drop it will you start feeling the relief from the pain. You can only control your actions. To create the peace you desire, allowing yourself to forgive will be the best comfort and you will start to heal.

A person's actions have more to do with the internal battle that they are struggling with than it has to do with you. Understanding this will help you lean towards compassion and grace. Hurt people will hurt people. We all make mistakes. God loves and has grace for us, we can let the love of God shine through and have that grace for others.

With all of that being said I want to talk about ensuring healthy boundaries. With my sense of confidence came clear expectations to others as well. I expect mutual respect. I wouldn't do things to them and I do not want them done to me. There are several things I will no longer tolerate. Just to name a few, I will not tolerate someone being degrading or belligerent to me. I will not tolerate someone taking advantage of me or lying to me. I have had several situations where this needed to be expressed. If appropriate it was discussed before it was an issue but in some situations, I made it clear after it happened that I would not continue to tolerate it. With it continuing there have been parting of relationships but since they were unhealthy ones it was necessary and appropriate to create the distance with the healthy boundaries. I still think about those people and even keep them in my prayers but don't feel it is healthy to have them in my life. Having standards for what I will and will not tolerate continues to be a big part of taking care of myself and keeping genuine relationships and people as part of my circle.

"Don't blame a clown for acting like a clown, ask yourself why you keep going to the circus" -Unknown

As part of people-pleasing, you feel a sense of shame when telling someone no. Which makes us agree to do things we don't want to do like head-up fundraising committees or be a carpool driver. We struggle to make up excuses to get out of it but ultimately do it often with sometimes underlining grudges. So what if we just said "no" that's it, "no" say it with me. "NO" No is a sentence and response all by itself. You do not need to explain or follow up with anything. The first few times that you say it, you may feel bad or have the urge to justify it but stay strong and leave it at a no. Once you then get over the initial shock of doing it you will feel a sense of pride and freedom. The shackle of people-pleasing can come off. Then the next step is to get out of your own head and stop listening to the stories you're telling yourself now of what they are saying about you now that you said no. It doesn't matter. If they want to be mad or hold a grudge that is not your issue, that is theirs. We only have control over our actions and not over how others take our responses. So speak up, because you are worth it!

Chapter 10.

Seeing beauty in your reflection

I was not always a fan of what I would see when I looked in the mirror. For years I would focus on what others called flaws. I would nit-pick at myself from my hair all the way down to my toes but I always like my smile. Even at my heaviest I would always smile at myself and see the beauty in me. That didn't stop me from comparing myself to others around me though. I felt only if I was thinner then I would be happier. I would feel deep down that my weight is what was holding me back. I put a lot of my self-worth in a number on the scale and the circumference of my waist.

I knew I was heavy but I did not see it as apparent when I looked in the mirror as when I saw a photo of myself. I am very grateful for that actually. Because even though the clothes tag said 3x I would smile as I tried it on. I have said and practiced for years every time you try on clothes ESPECIALLY a swimsuit, take a moment and smile at yourself in the mirror. Everything is going to look crappy on you if you try it on with a grouchy look on your face. When you smile at yourself you will see the good and pick the clothes that make you feel better and more confident. Then when you buy that outfit and wear it you will remember the way it made you feel and stand a little taller. I always say confidence is the best accessory to any outfit! We have all seen people wear outfits that we could never dream of wearing in public yet they are rocking them because they are wearing them with confidence!

I know what it is like walking into a room knowing you are the heaviest woman. The looks that I got I would start to internalize and then the stories would start in my head, but I would try to quiet those stories and hold my head higher just feeling proud to be there. I would still compare myself to others but comparison really does lead to sadness, self-shame, and destructive thoughts. It would be a slope that I would find myself on often but had to continue to tell myself that I was worthy and I had great qualities that went far beyond my dress size.

The people that make and purchase plus-size clothing for the stores need to have a wake-up call. Not all large women are old, floral is horrible and horizontal stripes are not our friends! Finding cute clothes was a hard task on top of finding ones that would fit! I would see the size on the tag, try it on and be so disappointed when it was too small. I can't be the next size bigger I would think to myself! Then either put it back on the rack with my self-worth at a new low or squeeze into the size thinking it's not too bad and when I lose a few pounds it will fit better. Why do we do this to ourselves? No one sees the size tag on our clothing but they can see when it is too tight! Find the clothes that fit you, you feel good in, and that are comfortable. Don't find the clothes that you can fit in.

I was so self-conscious that for years I would not wear tank tops or shorts! It would be 100 degrees outside and there I was, sweating in a t-shirt and pants. It wasn't until my late 20's when I bought my first tank top! The feeling of bare arms was both freeing and scary. I told myself countless stories of how people were staring at me and judging me. Now I realize just that, they were stories. The facts are no one was making any comments so what did it matter? Come to think of it, even if they did make a comment, I shouldn't have allowed it to affect me. But obviously, I kept myself inside of this low self-worth and self-esteem prison for far too long.

A few years ago I embarked on a journey to take back my health. In turn, becoming healthy finally allowed me to lose the weight I had been so desperately trying to lose my whole life. I have since gone on to lose over 110 pounds. It has been a transformation! Coming to learn it wasn't about a number on a scale of what I lost but it was about what gained in that process. I gained self-love, self-worth, self-esteem, and self-confidence. I now wear tank tops regularly and don't care one bit that my arms are not ripped. I have some extra skin when I wave but I own it and it makes me happy!

I worked hard and earned every extra ounce of skin that is on me since it used to be filled with fat and I am now healthy.

How is it that so many people lose weight and still do not find happiness? Again, happiness comes from within. When you put your value on a number on a scale you allow something external to define you. So many diets are deprivation of food, with this consistent practice the number on the scale drops. Even though we see the changes in the size of clothing we can wear we do not see a change in the mirror. We don't feel a change from within. People might compliment and say you are looking good but you are not feeling as good as you thought you would. Why is that? Because even though you have been cutting back on the food and exercising more you have not been feeding your soul with the love, compassion, encouragement, and motivation you need. You have not taken the time to care for and appreciate your body in all the stages that it is in and has gone through.

When we plant a seed in the garden we set out to do everything we can to ensure successful growth. As we see the sprout rise from the dirt we spend the time to ensure it is protected by the elements. It receives plenty of sunlight, providing water and nutrients in the soil. We continue to care for the plant as it gets bigger and starts to bloom. We need to do the same for ourselves if we want to change how we look at ourselves. Without working on what is on the inside we will never value and love what is on the outside regardless of the number on the scale or the size pants we wear.

For years my mom would set her goals based on the number on the scale. So often she would say when I lose 100 pounds I will travel or when I lose 100 pounds I am going to do this or buy that. Over the years she would yo-yo diet. Often she got close to the one-hundred-pound mark but self-sabotage would kick in and she would gain the weight back. Years have gone by and none of the things that she wanted to do or said she was going to do, she has actually done. So often we hold ourselves back and even place our lives on hold until we feel we are worthy of living it based on that number on the scale.

This process of loving our body can start today, right now! Take some time, think about and write down 10 things (yes 10) that you love and appreciate about the body you have right now. This is not as hard as some may think. When I do my yoga practice I reflect on this exercise often. An example is as I lay on my back with legs straight up, I twirl my ankles and wiggle my toes, I take a moment to admire my feet. They get me to where I want to go. I have the gift of mobility. I love my feet and all they do for me.

1. _____
2. _____
3. _____
4. _____
5. _____
6. _____
7. _____
8. _____
9. _____
10. _____

Our bodies are incredible. They do so much for us that we take it for granted. Like so many things we don't appreciate it until we no longer have it. Several years ago I broke my foot. I had to have surgery and was on crutches for months. The lack of mobility was so frustrating even the little tasks in life that I could no longer do. Once my foot healed, I looked at my feet and the ability to go for a walk in a whole new way, it is a gift.

Every day we are bombarded with advertisements for the latest beauty products. Whatever society is calling beautiful there is a product or procedure to get you there. Marketing is feeding us the lie that beauty is only skin deep. We are made to feel we need their product and without it, we are not beautiful. If we are all made to be authentic and unique then why is it so important for us to all buy the same products? Because that is business, that is how the companies make money. So before you get sucked into thinking you are less beautiful without the product, take a moment and ask yourself is this what I want or am I being sucked in by marketing?

Wouldn't it be wonderful if when we looked at people we looked for their beauty from within? We can actually do this, beauty is in the eye of the beholder. Have you ever noticed someone can become more or less attractive the more you get to know them? This has been the case with numerous people that I have met over the years. At first, I thought man, they are so attractive, but as I get to know them the spark quickly fades. They are not coming across as a very nice person, arrogant, or even cruel. I then see them as not attractive at all.

This has also gone the other way. My husband and I met on an online dating site back when they first became popular. My blackberry phone could not blow up his photo very large so I had no idea what he looked like before our first date. Our conversations leading up to that first date were incredible and I could not wait to meet this fantastic mystery man. As he walked up to me I thought he was handsome but not what I had pictured in my mind. We went on to have an incredible time. The more we were together the more I fell for him. As the years have gone on I find him to be the sexiest man alive, no celebrity can compare. Because I see the amazing soul and kind heart that he has. The way he makes me feel reflects the beauty I see in him.

Taking the time to stop and look at your own reflection is important. Go to the mirror, really look at yourself. Don't sit and criticize the wrinkles or the rolls but take the time to appreciate every wrinkle that came from a laugh and reflect that growing old is not a gift everyone is given. Look at your hands, all that they have done for you and been through over the years. Understand that this is your body, your face, your skin, and your hair and it is all a gift. Remember, you were created with that same beauty as the sunset. Now smile because you have so much to honor and be proud of. See the good. See the gift and stop using negative self-talk. I invite you from now on every time you see yourself in the mirror take a moment and smile at yourself because we need to be our own biggest cheerleader.

Chapter 11.

You are what you eat

We've gone over the way we think about ourselves, talk to ourselves, look at ourselves but now let's talk about what we feed ourselves. Things that are toxic and damaging come from what we feed ourselves mentally and physically but it wasn't until a few years ago I put this correlation together.

For years I tried countless diets. I could remember as a kid, drinking those nasty weight loss shakes hoping they would help. I would try so many weight loss pills, attend support meetings, mail order products, and prepackaged foods. I would count calories, measure, track and weigh everything I put into my mouth. Only to attend a weekly weight loss meeting and have the lady weigh me in say I gained then ask in an attempt to care if I expected to gain. I would feel the lump of disappointment in my throat and hunger in my stomach as I sat down to hear about their greatest new product that I needed to buy that would be the answer to my problems. I loved food and eating so it is no wonder I could not stick to and find success with deprivation diets. Depriving yourself of food is like depriving yourself of air; there is only a matter of time before your instincts kick in and you start gasping. You start eating, so we need to understand there is a difference between what we are eating to fuel our body and just feeding ourselves

A few years ago when everyone was raving about the low carb high fat and high protein diets I thought why not try it. It gave me a pass to eat the double bacon cheeseburger. All I had to do was leave it off the bun...ok whatever I could do to lose weight. So I did it. I lost about twenty-five pounds so I thought this was finally the answer to provide the weight loss I had been so desperately wanting. Approximately four months into eating this way I started getting really bad foot pain that then led to leg pain and numbness in both of my legs from the knees down. I was losing clumps of my hair and had an intense dry mouth. I would feel my heart palpitating and get shortness of breath for no reason. It progressed to the point when I started having issues with speech. I could think of words but could not spit them out. I was having memory issues and asking the same questions without realizing I had already asked the question or heard the answer. I sought medical attention and after thousands of dollars worth of tests, the doctors had no idea what was wrong with me. But offered me a prescription for my symptoms.

Our society is so quick to take medication to resolve a symptom but the symptom is a warning sign something is wrong in our body. If the engine light came on in our car would we put a piece of tape over it and keep driving? No, we would fix the problem or we would expect our engine to blow up! Then why are we so accepting that a pill will fix us when it is only masking the issue? I had to find the answer as to what was really going on with me.

This was shortly after the time I embarked on my relationship with the Lord so I prayed for help, healing, and guidance. I asked God to show me what to do and what would help. As God always does, he provided. I came across a suggestion to watch a plant-based food documentary. Feeling the Hippocrates quote of "Let food be thy medicine" I watched it. It opened up a world that I never embarked on before...actual health! Weight loss is the byproduct of being healthy, it is not the other way around! Learning the science behind the whole food plant-based way of eating was mind-blowing and at the same time intimidating.

Whole food plant-based is in essence healthy vegan. What you eat consists of unprocessed or minimally processed foods and plant-based so what comes out of the earth including vegetables, fruit, grains, beans, legumes, nuts, and seeds. It excludes all animal products including meat, fish, eggs, and dairy. I had heard of vegetarians and vegans before but in our small town, I never met a vegan! We're in Wisconsin, known for cows and cheese is the main food group. It was a lot to take in. I watched a few more documentaries and doctor lectures digging into the science behind health and this way of eating. I was convinced. This was a path I had never been on before. I no longer had to count calories or measure my food. All I had to do was eat what grew from the earth and I could eat as much as I wanted? OK, I was on board since I always was a fan of many fruits and vegetables and felt this was something worth trying.

I told my husband my plan. He was supportive but was not on board to do it with me. At first, I switched to vegan but within the first week, I was eating potato chips, onion rings, and Oreos.

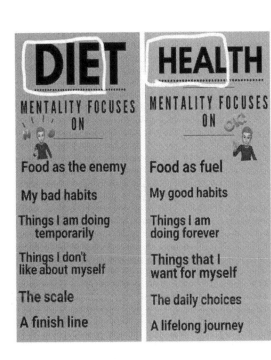

Knowing that those food choices were not about health I went full whole food plant-based. I was the one in our family that grocery shopped and cooked for the family. Even though my husband and son were not switching to this way of eating I could not in good conscience buy and cook the toxins that I have now learned is in countless food products in the grocery store. My husband and I came to a wonderful agreement. He'd be ok having only plant-based meals at home but when we went out to dinner they could order whatever they wanted and I would keep my thoughts to myself. So that is what we did and it worked great for our family.

Every time I prepared a meal I felt I was feeding myself and my family love and nutrients. Being able to eat all I wanted was such a treat. I found the transition to be easy. The first week turned into a month. Soon the bizarre symptoms that I was having started to go away. I started to feel more alive. Within my research, I would hear people say they feel more energetic when eating this way. I started to experience it, but it was not about having energy like needing to go for a run around the block (still don't find that appealing) but I started to feel lighter like bouncy. Six weeks after completely switching my way of eating all of my symptoms were gone. The weight was coming off with no effort since my body was healing and becoming healthier. I realized when you eat life you feel more alive but when I would eat death I would feel lethargic and sluggish.

When seeing these fantastic changes I needed to learn more and became completely submerged in anything I could read, watch or listen to plant-based related. Some would say I became a little obsessed but I felt every time I took a bite of something I was either loving myself or harming myself and I wanted to become more educated about what was in our foods and what I was putting into my body. I wanted to keep choosing love and life.

I could stay strong and always choose vegan options if I was in a situation where options were limited, but sugar and refined carbs like bread and pasta would quietly call my name. I then dove in, discovered, and researched food addictions. Did you know sugar is more addictive than cocaine? No wonder why it is so hard to say no! Yet people understanding and respecting food addiction is not socially accepted. Think about it, if you had a cocaine addiction that you were battling and went to a family event grandma would not pressure you to do a line with her. Yet, if you tell people that you are not eating sugar and explain addiction you are asked to make an exception because grandma made your favorite cookies!

The road of taking back my health has been a twisting and turning one. About nine months into my journey I still felt something was a little off. I decided to seek help from a holistic nutritional therapist. She found I was low in several vitamins and minerals. I ate every color of the rainbow of fruits and vegetables daily, how was I not getting enough vitamins? After testing it was discovered I had an intestinal parasite. What, gross right? It was unknown how long I had been letting this life sucker hitch a ride but it was the cause of my vitamin deficiency and ongoing brain fog that I was experiencing.

With this knowledge, I started researching gut health! Scientists say our gut is our second brain. If our gut is not happy and healthy neither are we. Signs of your gut not being happy are bloating, gas, constipation, diarrhea, heartburn, skin irritations, and more!

For years I would have massive acid reflux, I was diagnosed with GERD and given a pill to stop the acid in my stomach. I took that pill for a long time with some relief but my acid reflux actually stopped when I switched to eating whole food plant-based. I discontinued using the medication shortly after making the switch and have not had an issue since. Fast forward to learning about my gut health, I was just masking the symptoms to what was really going on in my body.

To keep your gut happy your good gut bacteria feeds on fiber so I was doing good with all of the food I have been eating. But I then set out to ensure I took care of my good gut bacteria while working to eliminate the bad and evicting the parasites. With a slow holistic approach, I was able to eradicate the parasites that were affecting my health. Soon after they were gone my brain fog lifted and I became more regular in the bathroom. I no longer need to take the additional supplements since I can feed myself and absorb the nutrients my body needs.

It has been a few years since I switched to a plant-based way of eating. I have lost a lot of weight and gotten my health back. It continues to be a process daily to make good choices. The biggest key is consistency. You can't eat a salad once a week and then eat processed garbage out of a package full of chemicals and wonder why you are having issues with your health.

Loving yourself with what we put on our fork is so important. We are worthy of life, love, and nutrition not the chemical addiction of the toxins then use the term "treating yourself" to justify consuming the poison that will hurt our bodies and fog our brains. I recall going to a family celebration and my well-intended brother-in-law asked if I was allowing myself a cheat day so I could treat

myself to all the food there. I knew what he was meaning but the concept was hard for me to wrap my brain around. With all that I have learned about what is in most foods we consume and the harm that it does to our bodies the thought of eating it no longer came across as a treat. It felt more like harm and I was able to easily say no.

Emotional eating and food addiction continue to play a role in my life. I am far from perfect but I am much more aware of what I am putting in my body and can see and feel the effects when I eat processed foods and sugars. I actually become more irritable after eating processed sugar, especially licorice. I have found licorice is my horrible drug. I can smell it through the package and if I eat one, I binge eat the whole package. My stomach will start hurting and I become lethargic for a few days afterward. My mood is even different after I eat it. This is NOT a TREAT! Never before in my life was I aware of how food affected me other than when it changed the number on the scale but now, I can feel and see it in so many other ways.

When we focus on our health we can make the right choice to love ourselves with what we choose to put into our mouth.

Chapter 12.

It's time to Become Redeemed

Redeemed means to be set free, you no longer have to perform or live in the shadows of your past. Your past no longer defines you and you no longer live there. You are a new creation when you become redeemed. As you are walking forward in life, no matter how far off the path you've gone you can always come back, starting with the next step. This has been the overall theme of my entire life in so many areas. So when people ask me "have you always been so damn happy?" My answer is no because I am now redeemed.

As we learn who we are, overcome challenges and see a better way; it is important and so rewarding to reach out and help those on the same type of path that is not too far behind. We can be a light and an inspiration to those who are stumbling to find their way. Throughout my journey people have come to me asking questions, seeking inspiration, and looking for guidance. I love to be the voice of encouragement, positivity, and honesty for others.

As I answered my calling to get into coaching I had to first understand what it really was and how it was different from therapy or counseling. Therapy and counseling are wonderful professional supports to help create stabilization within mental health needs. Coaching is focused on helping a person mobilize in their life. Take action steps, discover their road map, address the roadblocks, and unleash their insights to overcome and conquer their goals.

I quickly learned that despite me being new into the coaching world this was a fast-growing industry and there were countless coaches out there advertising their services. So what would set me apart? I really gave that question a lot of thought. Since no two people are alike then no two coaching practices are alike. I am honest, sincere, and genuine. I don't just talk the talk because I have lived in the valleys of life and worked to climb and overcome the mountains.

Launching my Redeemed Coaching is more than just a business, it is my passion, my heart, and my soul that is poured out to everyone I get to work with. The love, attention, and encouragement that I have for my clients is inspiring and shown to be life-changing.

There are different avenues within Redeemed Coaching.

One on One- I work one on one virtually with individuals to discuss their journey and goals then recognize where they are holding themselves back or feeling stuck. We then work together to address and implement action steps to overcome their hurdles so they can achieve all that they have been created to be.

Group Coaching- Continuous groups of like-minded and common goal individuals come together in a group coach setting. We meet virtually to complete workshops and set tasks to reach their goals.

Redeemed Eating- A fun and fulfilling entity of Redeemed Coaching. It is a group coaching platform centered around whole food plant-based eating. Meeting virtually weekly discussing topics such as emotional eating and food addiction. Helping others transition into this way of eating with meal plans and interactive cooking classes.

Redeemed Retreat- Encompasses all of the self-love entities discussed in this book. I host an in-person event for small groups. It is a four-day, three-night retreat. Guests stay at the resort. I create an itinerary with custom activities including personalized yoga, provide plant-based meals, teach interactive cooking classes, lead personal development workshops and other creative activities to ensure your time at the retreat is relaxing and you leave with a sense of feeling redeemed.

When I set out on my personal development and transformation journey I never imagined it would lead to where it is now. I have become a mentor, leader, and coach for so many amazing people that have gone on to do amazing and inspiring things. Telling my story and sharing my journey I was encouraged by so many to write a book to share my wisdom and experiences. So here I am, now a published author! I have been a guest speaker on several coaching, entrepreneur, and plant-based podcast shows. It just confirms when you put your mind to something you can accomplish it and the only thing holding you back is your own thoughts!

I would love to hear from you and meet you. Please contact me at my website www.RedeemedCoaching.com

Let me ask you, does your life feel overwhelming and everything is unpredictable? You enjoyed reading this information but you can't seem to shut your mind off, even when you are sleeping. You are trapped in your own negative thoughts. This is not the life you signed up for, right?

It's time to hit the reset button.

I have created a 21-day Mindset Reset Challenge to change the way you think of yourself! Every day for 21 days, you will learn a new technique to help you be more calm, grounded, and centred. So, are you ready to meet yourself and hear more about this amazing opportunity?

Visit the 21 day Mindset Reset Challenge on my website for more details…

https://www.redeemedcoaching.com/21-day-mindset-reset-challenge

21 Day Mindset Reset Challenge — Redeemed Coaching: Body, Mind, Soul - life change coaching

What Kristi's Clients are Saying

"Before I found Kristi I had no idea where to even begin with my business. I didn't even really know if I could sustain a business! I felt like I had no one to talk to that genuinely cared about my life or success, let alone someone that was willing to help me move forward. After we started working together, her coaching and accountability helped me land multiple clients, build genuine relationships, and have confidence in myself that I never knew I could attain. Our time together has made such an impact on my life that my business, relationships and self-esteem continue to improve every day. The bond we share is unlike any other. I can't thank you enough."

-Emily L.

"What a great experience I had working with Kristi as a coach. I got so much insight on a better way of thinking. Instead of what I have to do, I think now what I get to do and focus on what I have to share with people. She was very patient as well as an amazing active listener who made me feel like I was being heard while giving wonderful suggestions. If I could have her as a lifetime coach I would. Thank you so much for allowing me to have this educational journey with you by my side. If anyone needs great support, motivation, and guidance I would highly recommend reaching out to Kristi immediately!"

-Brian T

"Since working with Kristi so much in my life has changed and all for the good. I feel such a sense of confidence and pride. She is always so kind and supportive. She helps me see things in a different light."

- Cheyenne D.

"I wasn't even sure I needed a coach, but I decided to go for it because I was stuck and Kristi was already helping me think about things differently during the intro session I had with her. I sure am glad I decided to coach with her! Within the first week of working with her, I doubled the amount of money I'd made so far in my own business this year. She helped me think about things differently, and it made a HUGE difference in my life. If you're not sure if you need a coach, you should definitely go for it. It will be more than worth your time."

- Abigail W.

"The connection Kristi and I have is amazing. I know I can talk to her about anything with zero judgement. She encourages me and tells me the truth even if I am not sure if I want to hear it. I see myself in a different light. The love and pride I now have for myself is what I have always been searching for. I am so happy that I found Kristi and I get to call her my coach. Even my family and co-workers have seen the change in me. I feel less anxious and stressed. Knowing Kristi is always there for me means so much. Thank you Kristi for all you are."

-Jennifer R.

"Kristi is such a joy to work with. She is full of knowledge and wisdom. What comes through most is her heart for people. She is supportive and genuinely wants to be a part of my life. She is always there anytime I need. I'm so happy I found Kristi to work with. She makes me feel like I can and will succeed."

- Tammy D.

"Kristi has been an inspiration and so helpful. I couldn't do it alone but with her support I feel like I can tackle anything!"

- Sarah R.

About the Author

Kristi Davis, her husband Jason, and son Apollo

Growing up in a small town in central Wisconsin I was raised to know what work was and the value of a dollar. I would relate my childhood similar to the 90's sitcom Roseanne. We didn't have much money but with my parents' strong work ethic they never had us go without the basics. We lived in the country surrounded by farm fields. My older sister and I were best friends and always looked out for each other. There was love in our home but with my parents working long hours there were high expectations of us as children, which helped us become very independent. At the age of twelve, I started my first job at a local restaurant and have been working hard ever since. My parents were always pushing us to make good choices and be the best we could be. Throughout this book, I share a lot of my journey to lead me to where I am today. I am now happily married living on a lake property in northern Wisconsin. Hard work, determination, faith and never giving up have shown time and time again that anything is possible and it is never too late to follow your dreams.

How to contact the Author

I encourage you to visit my website www.RedeemedCoaching.com There you will find more information about my services, schedule a virtual meeting with me.

Email: Kristi@RedeemedCoaching.com

Facebook: Kristi Davis- Redeemed Coaching. Body Mind Soul | Facebook

Instagram:Kristi Davis- Redeemed (@kristidavisredeemedhealthcoach) • Instagram photos and videos

One More Thing Before You Go...

I f you enjoyed reading this book or found it useful, I'd be very grateful if you'd post a short review on Amazon. Your support really does make a difference, and I read all the reviews personally, so I can get your feedback and make this book even better.

If you would like to leave a review, then all you need to do is click the review link on Amazon here:
https://amzn.to/3ychYU8

And if you live in the UK, you can leave it here:
https://amzn.to/3muBhpz

Thanks again for your support!

Manufactured by Amazon.ca
Bolton, ON

21801860R00044